Football

JOKES

Knock, knock . . .
Who's there?
Jane.
Jane who?
Jane who did the
drawings in this book.

(That's Jane Eccles, who loves drawing
and works in a tiny room in her house
in Hampshire, where she lives with her
husband and son and small grey cat.)

Also available from
Macmillan Children's Books

The Bumper Book of Very Silly Jokes

Christmas Jokes

Football

JOKES

Fantastically funny
jokes for football
fanatics

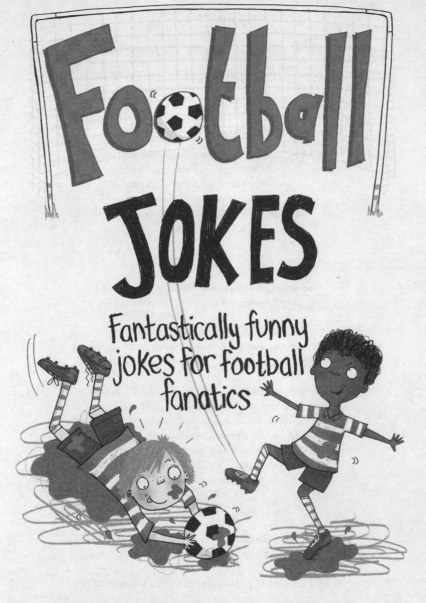

Illustrated by Jane Eccles

MACMILLAN CHILDREN'S BOOKS

For Theo,
who prefers rugby to football,
but will like the critters in this book

First published 2014 by Macmillan Children's Books
a division of Macmillan Publishers Limited
20 New Wharf Road, London N1 9RR
Basingstoke and Oxford
Associated companies throughout the world
www.panmacmillan.com

ISBN 978-1-4472-5461-4

Text copyright © Macmillan Children's Books 2014
Illustrations copyright © Jane Eccles 2014

The right of Jane Eccles to be identified as the
illustrator of this work has been asserted by her in accordance
with the Copyright, Designs and Patents Act 1988.

1 3 5 7 9 8 6 4 2

A CIP catalogue record for this book is available from
the British Library.

Printed and bound by CPI Group (UK) Ltd, Croydon CR0 4YY

Contents

Kick-Off

What can light up a dull evening?
A football match.

What goes stomp, stomp, stomp, squelch?
An elephant with wet football boots.

DAD: How did this window get broken?

TOMMY: Er, my football took a shot at goal while I was cleaning it.

Young Alec came off the pitch looking very dejected and slunk into the dressing room.

'I've never played so badly before,' he sighed.

'Oh,' answered a fellow player. 'You've played before, have you?'

TEACHER: And why were you late for school today, Jimmy?

JIMMY: I was dreaming about a football match and they went into extra time.

A tourist visiting London stopped a man carrying a football and asked, 'How do I get to Wembley?'

'Practice,' was the reply.

How can you stop moles digging up the football pitch?

Hide their spades.

MOTHER MONSTER: Why don't you go out and play football with your little brother?

LITTLE MONSTER: Oh, Mum, I'd much rather play with a real football.

Why was the mummy no good at football?

He was too wrapped up in himself.

What did the pitch say to the player?
'I hate it when people treat me like dirt.'

What's the difference between the
Prince of Wales and a throw-in?
One's heir to the throne; the other's
thrown to the air.

MOTHER: David! It's time to get up! It's 8.15!
DAVID: Who's winning?

Which former Manchester
United player never scored a goal?
George Worst.

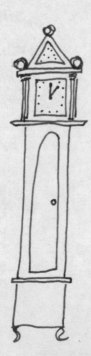

When is a footballer like
a grandfather clock?
When he's a striker.

When are footballers like babies?
When they dribble.

When is a kick like a boat?
When it's a punt.

What happened when
the boy footballer married
a girl footballer?
*People said it was
a perfect match.*

How do you stop a hot
and sweaty footballer
from smelling?
Put a peg on his nose.

What's large, grey and carries a
trunk and two pairs of football boots?
An elephant that's just joined the team.

What do you do if you're too
hot at a football match?
Sit next to a fan.

What did the ball say to the footballer?
'I get a kick out of you.'

HARRY: Every night I dream about football –
of running down the pitch, passing the ball,
avoiding tackles . . .
LARRY: Don't you ever dream about girls?
HARRY: What? And miss a chance at goal?

Why are there fouls in football?
Same reason there are ducks in cricket.

KEN: I've just been to the doctor and he said I can't play football.

BEN: Oh? When did he see you play?

Why can't horses play football?
Because they've got two left feet.

Which footballer sails down the field like a yacht?
Gary Spinnaker.

Which fish is a famous ex-footballer?

Finny Jones.

The doctor was giving members of the team a medical.

'Breathe out three times,' he said to one of the players.

'Are you checking my lungs?' asked the player.

'No, I'm going to clean my spectacles,' replied the doctor.

How can a footballer stop his nose running?

Put out a foot and trip it up.

How does an
octopus go on to
a football pitch?
Well-armed!

Why was the centipede no use
to the football team?

*He never arrived on the pitch until half-time –
it took him so long to lace up his boots.*

Which animal plays
football standing on
its head?
Yoga Bear.

What two things should a footballer never eat before breakfast?

Lunch and dinner.

What's black and white and wears dark glasses?

A football in disguise.

What happens to the boy who misses the bus home from the match?

He catches it when he gets home.

Two flies were playing football in a saucer.
One said to the other, 'We'll have to do better
than this – we're playing in the cup next week!'

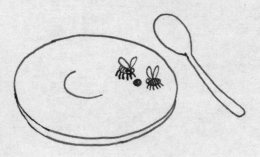

What happened when a herd of
cows had a football match?
There was udder chaos.

What can a footballer never make right?
His left foot.

How do ghost footballers keep fit?

With regular exorcise.

What's the difference between a flea-ridden dog and a bored football spectator?

One's going to itch; the other's itching to go.

What has two feet like a footballer, two eyes like a footballer and two arms like a footballer, yet isn't a footballer?

A photograph of a footballer.

How do you hire a professional footballer?

Stand him on a chair.

Team Spirit

Which football team never
meets before a match?
Queen's Park Strangers.

Which football team
should you not eat
in a sandwich?
Oldham.

GILL: My dog can play football.

BILL: Really? What a clever animal!

GILL: Oh, I don't know. When he plays for the local team it usually loses.

LENNY: The Leeds manager said I'd make a great footballer if it weren't for two things.

BENNY: What were they?

LENNY: My feet.

MR GREEN: I've been invited to join the firm's football team. They want me to play for them very badly.

MR BROWN: In that case, you're just the man.

Manchester United was playing Chelsea at Stamford Bridge. A man wearing a bright red and white rosette walked up to the ticket office and asked the price of admission.

'Twenty pounds, sir,' said the attendant.

'Here's ten pounds,' replied the man. 'There's only one team worth watching.'

SCOTTISH TEAM CAPTAIN: How can we raise the level of our game?
SCOTTISH TEAM MANAGER: Play at the top of Ben Nevis?

What's yellow, has twenty-two legs and peels off at half time?
Banana United.

After the match the team was in the dressing-room when the trainer came in and asked if anyone had seen his spectacles.

'Yes,' replied one of the players. 'They were out on the pitch.'

'Then why didn't you bring them in?' asked the trainer.

'I didn't think you'd want them after everyone had trodden on them,' replied the player.

The architect was showing the team round the new stadium.

'I think you'll find it hasn't got a flaw,' he said proudly.

'What do we walk on then?' asked one of the players.

FIRST PLAYER: Wasn't the captain angry when you said you were leaving the team next month?

SECOND PLAYER: Yes. He thought it was this month.

Which member of
the team flies
down the field?
The winger.

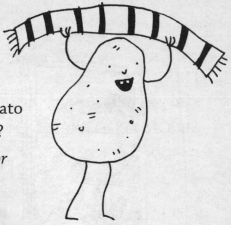

Why did the potato
go to the match?
*So it could root for
the home team.*

What position did the ducks
play in the football team?
Right and left quack.

Which football team comes
out of an ice-cream van?
Aston Vanilla.

Which London team keeps its boots in the fridge?
Tottenham Coldspur.

Which football team spends all
its spare time at pop concerts?
Blackburn Ravers.

MRS ROUND: I hear your son has a place in the
school football team. What position does he play?
MRS LONG: I think he's one of the drawbacks.

A man went to meet the members of a vegetable football team.

'This stick of celery is our goalie, the carrots are our centre forwards and the onions are our backs,' explained his host.

'And what's that one over there, telling everyone else what to do?' the man asked, pointing to a mud-covered vegetable that was lounging around.

'Oh, him?' replied the host. 'He's our coach potato.'

A man was up in court charged with trying to set fire to Chelsea's grandstand.

When questioned by the judge he said he had a burning interest in football.

What team is good in an omelette?
Best Ham.

Which Midlands team shrank and
became known as the clump of trees?
Notts Forest.

What was the monkey in the
team especially good at?
Banana shots.

FIRST PLAYER: Why did you call the team captain Camera?

SECOND PLAYER: Because he's always snapping at me.

If it takes twenty men six months to build a grandstand at the football pitch, how long would it take forty men to build it?

No time at all, because the twenty men had already completed it!

DON: How's the new player coming along?
RON: He's trying.
DON: I've heard he's very trying.

When Harry retired
from the team he said
he was going to work in
a bank.

'Why do you want to do
that?' asked Larry.

'I've heard there's money in
it,' replied Harry.

MANAGER: This dressing room is disgusting! It hasn't been cleaned for a month!

CLEANER: Don't blame me. I've only been here for a fortnight.

Why did the elephant paint his toenails red?

So he could hide in a pile of Arsenal shirts.

Why did the elephant wear a red-and-white shirt?
So he could play for Arsenal.

Will was rather underweight and
was told by his doctor that he'd be
a better footballer if he put on a
few pounds. 'Tell you what,' said
the doctor. 'Eat a plum. If you
swallow it whole you'll gain
a stone.'

What do you call a noisy football fan?
A foot-bawler.

Why did the manager have the pitch flooded?
He wanted to bring his sub.

'Football, football,' sighed Mrs Jones. 'That's all you think of. I bet you don't even remember when we got married.'

'I certainly do,' said Mr Jones. 'It was the day Arsenal beat West Ham six–nil.'

What happened when the footballer went to see his doctor to complain about flat feet?

The doctor gave him a bicycle pump.

JOHN: My mum says she'll leave my dad if he doesn't stop watching football.

TOM: Oh dear. That would be awful.

JOHN: Yes. Dad says he'll really miss her.

PE TEACHER: Andy, you're hopeless at football, cricket and tennis. I don't think you'll ever be first at anything.

ANDY: I'm always first in the dinner queue, sir.

What goes in pink and comes out blue?

A footballer who plays for a team that only has cold showers.

FELICITY: While Darren was taking a shower after the match, someone stole all his clothes.

TRACEY: Oh dear! What did he come home in?

FELICITY: The dark!

TALENT SCOUT: Your number six looks as if he might be a good footballer if his legs weren't so short.

TEAM MANAGER: They're not that short. They do both reach the floor.

Why did the footballer put his bed in the fireplace?

He wanted to sleep like a log.

Knock, Knock on the Dressing-Room Door

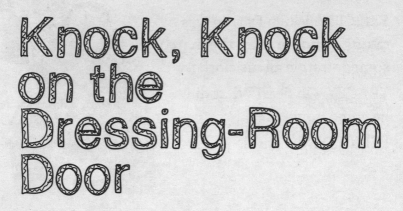

Knock, knock.

Who's there?

Aladdin.

Aladdin who?

Aladdin the street's waiting for
you to come out and play football.

Knock, knock.
Who's there?
Alison.
Alison who?
Alison to the football results
on the radio.

Knock, knock.
Who's there?
Euripides.
Euripides who?
Euripides football shorts and
you buy me a new pair.

Knock, knock.
Who's there?
Godfrey.
Godfrey who?
Godfrey tickets for the
match on Saturday.

Knock, knock.
Who's there?
Kerry.
Kerry who?
Kerry me off the pitch –
I think my leg's broken.

Knock, knock.
Who's there?
Juno.
Juno who?
Juno what time the kick-off is?

Knock, knock.
Who's there?
Al B.
Al B who?
Al B home straight after the match.

Knock, knock.
Who's there?
Howell.
Howell who?
Howell you take
that corner?

Knock, knock.
Who's there?
Weed.
Weed who?
Weed like to win this game.

Knock, knock.
Who's there?
Ammonia.
Ammonia who?
Ammonia little boy and
I can't run as fast as you.

Knock, knock.
Who's there?
Ida.
Ida who?
Ida terrible time getting to the match –
all the buses were full.

Knock, knock.
Who's there?
Money.
Money who?
Money hurts since I
twisted it on the pitch.

Knock, knock.

Who's there?

Harvey.

Harvey who?

Harvey going to have another game before lunch?

Knock, knock.

Who's there?

Stu.

Stu who?

Stu late to score a goal now.

Knock, knock.
Who's there?
Waiter.
Waiter who?
Waiter minute
while I tie my
bootlaces.

Knock, knock.
Who's there?
Luke.
Luke who?
Luke, he's just scored a goal.

Knock, knock.
Who's there?
Oily.
Oily who?
Oily in the morning's the best time to train.

Knock, knock.
Who's there?
Saul.
Saul who?
Saul over when the final whistle blows.

Knock, knock.
Who's there?
Argo.
Argo who?
Argo to Elland Road
on Saturdays.

Knock, knock.
Who's there?
General Lee.
General Lee who?
General Lee I support Chelsea but
today I'm rooting for Fulham.

Knock, knock.

Who's there?

Farmer.

Farmer who?

Farmer birthday I got a
new pair of football boots.

Knock, knock.

Who's there?

Nana.

Nana who?

Nana your business who we put in goal.

Knock, knock.
Who's there?
Ken.
Ken who?
Ken Harry come out
and play football?

Knock, knock.
Who's there?
Hurd.
Hurd who?
Hurd my foot so I
couldn't play today.

Knock, knock.
Who's there?
Scold.
Scold who?
Scold wearing shorts to play football in winter.

Knock, knock.
Who's there?
Police.
Police who?
Police let me play with your new football.

Knock, knock.
Who's there?
Ammon.
Ammon who?
Ammon awfully good football player. Can I be in your team?

Knock, knock.
Who's there?
Omar.
Omar who?
Omar goodness, what a shot!

Knock, knock.
Who's there?
Macho.
Macho who?
Macho the Day.

Knock, knock.
Who's there?
Wanda.
Wanda who?
Wanda buy a new football?

Knock, knock.

Who's there?

Aardvark.

Aardvark who?

Aardvark to Scotland to see Celtic play.

Knock, knock.

Who's there?

Dozen.

Dozen who?

Dozen anyone in this village play football?

Knock, knock.
Who's there?
Gladys.
Gladys who?
Gladys Saturday – we can go to the match.

Knock, knock.
Who's there?
Stan.
Stan who?
Stan back – I'm going to shoot!

Knock, knock.
Who's there?
Philippa.
Philippa who?
Philippa bathtub –
I'm covered in mud.

Knock, knock.
Who's there?
Willy.
Willy who?
Willy score? Bet he won't!

Knock, knock.

Who's there?

Wayne.

Wayne who?

Wayne never stops when
I play football.

Knock, knock.

Who's there?

Snow.

Snow who?

Snow use, I'm going to
give you a red card.

Knock, knock.
Who's there?
Norma Lee.
Norma Lee who?
Norma Lee I play in goal but
today I'm at left back.

Knock, knock.
Who's there?
Althea.
Althea who?
Althea later,
down the club.

Knock, knock.
Who's there?
Buster.
Buster who?
Buster Old Trafford, please.

Knock, knock.
Who's there?
Ivan.
Ivan who?
Ivan new pair of boots – do you like them?

Knock, knock.
Who's there?
Ben.
Ben who?
Ben playing football today, have you?

Knock, knock.
Who's there?
Yolande.
Yolande who?
Yolande me some
money to get into
the match and I'll pay
you back next week.

Knock, knock.
Who's there?
Mister.
Mister who?
Mister bus, that's why
I'm late for the match.

Knock, knock.
Who's there?
Anna.
Anna who?
Anna rack keeps you warm after football.

Knock, knock.

Who's there?

Hammond.

Hammond who?

Hammond eggs are great after football.

Knock, knock.

Who's there?

Harriet.

Harriet who?

Harriet all my sandwiches – now I'm too weak to play!

Half-Time

Take a quick break from the golden game to catch up on your reading. Here are some of the titles in the club library.

Embarrassing Moments on the Pitch *by Lucy Lastic*

Twenty-five Years in Goal *by Annie Versary*

Will He Win? *by Betty Wont*

Let the Game Begin *by Sally Forth*

The Unhappy Fan *by Mona Lott*

The Poor Striker *by Miss D. Goal*

Why I Gave Up Football *by Arthur Itis*

Keep Trying Until the Final Whistle *by Percy Vere*

Heading the Ball *by I. C. Starrs*

We'll Win the Cup *by R. U. Sure*

Pre-Match-Night Nerves
by Eliza Wake

Keep Your Subs Handy
by Justin Case

Training Hard
by Xavier Strength

Buying Good Players
by Ivor Fortune

The New Player
by Izzy Anygood

Great Shot!
by Major Runn

Advertising the Match *by Bill Poster*

Which famous Liverpool
player was a sweeper?
Ian Brush.

Which football-team manager is
found in the greengrocer's?
Terry Vegetables.

A young football fan from Quebec
Once wrapped both his feet round
his neck.
Though he tried hard, he got
Tied up in a knot,
And now he's an absolute wreck.

DAD: Your school report is terrible. You've come bottom out of twenty in every subject. You're even bottom in football – and that's your favourite.

SON: It could be worse.

DAD: How?

SON: I'd be bottom out of thirty if I was in John's class. It's bigger.

A young football fan of Southend
Wrote in rhyme – several verses he penned,
Of their triumphs and glory,
Their total history –
It drove all his friends round the bend.

What's the best day for a footballer
to eat bacon and eggs for breakfast?
Fry-day.

Why did the footballer's dog
run away from home?
Doggone if I know!

ERIC: My doctor says I can't play football.
DEREK: Oh, so he's seen you play too, has he?

Why did the man become a marathon
runner instead of a footballer?
The doctor told him he had athlete's foot.

Why did the footballer
call his dog Carpenter?
*He was always doing little
jobs around the house.*

Two boys were walking past a house surrounded by a high wall when the owner came out holding a football. 'Is this your ball?' he demanded.

'Er, has it done any damage?' asked the first boy.

'No,' said the householder.

'Then it's ours,' said the second boy.

What position did Cinderella play in the football team?

Sweeper.

Why was Cinderella thrown out of the football team?

Because she kept running away from the ball.

Did you hear
about the
footballer who
had to lose weight? He went
on a coconut and banana diet.
He didn't lose any weight,
but he couldn't half
climb trees!

LARGE FOOTBALLER: My doctor put me
on a seafood diet.

SMALL FOOTBALLER: Really?

LARGE FOOTBALLER: Yes.
The more I see, the
more I eat.

FOOTBALLER: Doctor, will these little blue pills really make me a better player?

DOCTOR: I don't know, but no one I've given them to has ever come back.

BOSS: I thought you wanted the afternoon off to see your dentist.

MR BROWN: That's right.

BOSS: Then how come I saw you leaving the football ground with a friend?

MR BROWN: That was my dentist.

MUM: And was there a fight at the match again? You've lost your front teeth.

TOMMY: No I haven't. They're in my pocket.

A house was on fire, and a fireman called up to a woman trapped on the upper floor to throw down the baby she was holding.

'I can't, you might drop him!' screamed the woman.

'I won't, I used to be a professional footballer,' yelled the fireman.

So the woman threw down the baby, and the fireman headed him over the garden wall.

Two fleas were leaving a football match when it started to rain.

'Shall we walk?' asked the first flea.

'No,' said the second, 'let's take a dog.'

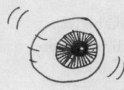 How can you tell when a footballer has a glass eye?

When it comes out in conversation.

It was Christmas time, and a little boy was being asked by his teacher about the Three Wise Men.

'Who were they?' asked the teacher.

'They were footballers,' replied the little boy.

'Whatever do you mean?' asked the teacher.

'Well, the carol says, "We three kings of Orient are . . ."'

LEN: Did you hear about the Italian footballer who belonged to a secret society that beat people up with shopping baskets?

KEN: No!

LEN: Yes. He was a member of the Raffia.

FIRST FOOTBALLER: Did you enjoy your massage?

SECOND FOOTBALLER: Oh yes. I like to feel kneaded.

Why did the doctor write on the footballer's toes?

To add a footnote.

Which footballer can jump higher than a house?

All of them – houses can't jump.

What was wrong with the footballer whose nose ran and feet smelt?

He was built upside down.

FOOTBALLER: I've a terrible pain in my right foot. What should I do?

PHYSIOTHERAPIST: Kick the ball with your left foot.

PARK-KEEPER: Why are you boys playing football in the trees?

RASHID AND MO: Because the sign says no ball games on the grass.

Why do ghosts play football?
For the ghouls, of course.

What do you call a press photographer
taking pictures of the match?
A flash guy.

Did you hear the story of the
peacock who played football?
It was a beautiful tail.

Own Goal

FIRST FOOTBALLER: How did you manage to break your leg?

SECOND FOOTBALLER: See those steps down to the car park?

FIRST FOOTBALLER: Yes

SECOND FOOTBALLER: I didn't.

Old Butterfingers had let five goals through in the first half.

'Can you spare me 10p?' he asked the captain. 'I want to phone a friend.'

'Here's 20p,' said the captain. 'Phone all your friends.'

GARY: I'm sorry I missed the goal. I could kick myself, I really could.

BARRY: Don't bother – you'd miss.

It was a cold, wet, miserable day and the goalie had had a bad match, allowing several goals through. As he sat moping in the dressing room, he sniffed and muttered, 'I think I've caught a cold.'

'Thank goodness you can catch something,' said the captain.

What gloves can a goalie see
and smell but not wear?

Foxgloves.

The goalie was so short-sighted he couldn't see the
ball until it was too late. A doctor friend prescribed
carrots to help his eyesight. The goalie ate lots of
carrots, but went back to the doctor a week later,
saying he still couldn't catch the ball because every
time he ran he now tripped over his ears.

What's the difference between a gutter
and a poor goalie?

One catches drops; the other drops catches.

What's the difference between a goalie
who's asleep and one who's awake?

With some goalies it's difficult to tell!

Did you hear about the player who threw away his boots because he thought they were sticking out their tongues at him?

Why did the idiot come on to the pitch
dressed in diving gear?
He'd been told he might be needed as a sub.

PE TEACHER: Now, Billy, you promised to practise hard at your football, didn't you?

BILLY: Yes.

PE TEACHER: And I promised to punish you if you didn't practise?

BILLY: Yes. But I don't mind if you break your promise.

GOALIE: Where shall we put the new player?

CAPTAIN: What's his name?

GOALIE: Robin Swallow.

CAPTAIN: Put him on the wing.

CAPTAIN: Why are you late for training?

PLAYER: I sprained my ankle.

CAPTAIN: That's a lame excuse.

DESHI: How old is your goalie?

HUAN: Approaching thirty.

DESHI: From which direction?

DANNY: Did you hear about the overweight player whose doctor put him on a diet that used a lot of olive oil?

ANNIE: Did he lose weight?

DANNY: No, but his knees don't creak any more.

Nobody ever passed the ball to Willy and he was moaning in the dressing room that he might as well be invisible.

'Who said that?' asked the captain.

FIRST VETERAN FOOTBALLER: How old are you?

SECOND VETERAN FOOTBALLER: Thirty-two. But I don't look it, do I?

FIRST VETERAN FOOTBALLER: No, but you used to.

Two young footballers were talking about the illnesses and accidents they had had.

'Once I couldn't walk for a year,' said the first.

'When was that?' asked the other.

'When I was a baby,' replied the first.

Old Harry had been retired from the game for many years, but he still liked to tell people how good he'd once been.

'They still remember me, you know,' he said. 'Only yesterday, when I was at the players' entrance, there were lots of press photographers queuing to take my picture.'

'Really?' said a disbelieving listener.

'Yes. And if you don't believe me, ask David Beckham – he was standing next to me.'

The great goalkeeper Jim 'Big Hands'
O'Reilly was walking down the street.

'I recognize that man,' said Ken. 'But
what's his name?'

'That's Big Hands,' replied Ben.

'Oh, really?'

'No, O'Reilly.'

Who's in goal when the ghost
team plays football?
The ghoulie, of course!

Why was the footballer
called Isaiah?

*Because one of his eyes was
'igher than the other.*

ANGRY NEIGHBOUR: Didn't you hear me banging
on your wall last night?

BLEARY-EYED NEIGHBOUR: No, but don't
worry – we had a bit of a party after the match and
were making quite a lot of noise ourselves.

Why was the ruler no good at football?

He just didn't measure up.

DARREN: Did you hear about the footballer who ate little bits of metal all day?

SHARON: No.

DARREN: It was his staple diet.

OLD FOOTBALL FAN: At last I've got my new hearing aid.

FRIEND: Does it work well?

OLD FAN: Half past three.

WAYNE: Why didn't you set a knife and fork for your brother when you laid the table?

JANE: Because Mum said that when he's been playing football he eats like a horse.

DANIEL: Mum, can I go out and play.

MUM: What, with those holes in your socks?

DANIEL: No, with Billy next door, he's got a new football.

Who ran out on the pitch when a player was injured and said, 'Miaow'?

The first aid kit.

Kitbag

What did the left football boot say to the right football boot?

'Between us we should have a ball.'

Who wears the biggest boots in the English team?

The player with the biggest feet.

Why can't a car play football?
Because it's only got one boot.

What do jelly babies wear
on their feet when they play
football?
Gumboots.

MUM: You've got your boots on the wrong feet.
ALEC: But, Mum, these are the only feet I've got.

What happens to football fans
who eat too many sweets?
They take up two seats.

What's the difference between an oak tree
and a tight football boot?

One makes acorns, the other makes corns ache.

DORIS: Did you hear the joke
about the dirty football shirt?

BORIS: No.

DORIS: That's one on you!

LITTLE TOMMY: I've looked everywhere for
my football boots and I can't find them.

TEACHER: Are you sure these aren't yours?
They're the only pair left.

LITTLE TOMMY: Quite sure. Mine had snow
on them.

MICKY: My brother's away training to be in a football team.

NICKY: Lucky thing! He must be quite grown up now.

MICKY: Yes. He wrote to us the other day saying he'd grown another foot, so my mum is knitting him an extra sock.

ANDY: Do you have holes in your football shorts?

BERTIE: No.

ANDY: Then how do you get them on?

A father asked his son what he'd like for Christmas.

'I've got my eye on that special football in the sports-shop window,' replied the lad.

'The thirty-five pound one?' asked his dad.

'That's right,' replied his son.

'You'd better keep your eye on it then, cos it's unlikely your boot will ever kick it,' said his dad firmly.

What wears out football boots but has no feet?
The ground.

Why did the footballer put corn in his boots?
He was pigeon-toed.

What did the football sock
say to the football boot?
'Well, I'll be darned!'

Young Chris was sent home from school to fetch
his football kit. When he returned later he was
wet through.

'Why are you all wet?'
asked the PE teacher.

'Sir, you said I must
go home to get my
kit, but it was in
the wash.'

FIRST SPIDER: I don't know what to get my husband for Christmas.

SECOND SPIDER: Give him what I gave mine – four pairs of football boots.

Why does a professional footballer always put his right boot on first?

It would be silly to put the wrong boot on, wouldn't it?

FIRST FOOTBALLER: Do you think it will rain for the match this afternoon?

SECOND FOOTBALLER: That depends on the weather, doesn't it?

OLDER BROTHER: Have you got your football boots on yet?

YOUNGER BROTHER: Yes, all but one.

What does a footballer part with but never give away?

His comb!

GILES: What's a football made of?

MILES: Pig's hide.

GILES: Why do they hide?

MILES: They don't. The pig's outside.

GILES: Then bring him in. Any friend of yours is a friend of mine.

CAPTAIN (looking at his watch): You should have been here at nine thirty.

LATE PLAYER: Why, what happened?

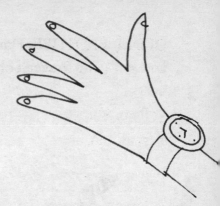

What runs around all day and lies at night with its tongue hanging out?

A football boot.

Two fans were discussing their packed lunches.

'What have you got?' asked Oli.

'Tongue sandwiches,' Eddie replied.

'Ugh, I couldn't eat something that had come out of an animal's mouth,' said Oli.

'What have you got then?' asked Eddie.

'Egg sandwiches.'

What can a footballer keep
even if he does give it away?
A cold!

INSURANCE AGENT:
This is a very good policy
sir. We pay up to £1,000
for broken arms and
legs.
DUMB FOOTBALLER:
But what do you do with
them all?

Why did the footballer stand on his head?
He was turning things over in his mind.

Why did the bald footballer
throw away his keys?
He'd lost all his locks.

Why was the snowman no good
playing in the big match?
He got cold feet.

Why did the player throw a bucket of water
on the pitch when he made his debut?
He wanted to make a big splash.

ANGRY NEIGHBOUR: I'll teach you
to kick footballs into my greenhouse!
NAUGHTY BOY: I wish you would, I
keep missing!

MOTHER: Why are you taking the baby's bib out with you, Tommy? I thought you were going to football practice?

TOMMY: Yes, but the coach said we'd be dribbling this week.

A group of neighbours was organizing a village friendly match followed by a picnic and realized they'd forgotten to invite the eccentric old lady who lived on the green. So they sent a child to invite her. 'It's no use now,' said the old lady, 'I've already prayed for rain.'

Mr Jones always got back late from football practice, and his wife got more and more fed up with keeping his supper warm and leaving him notes about it if she had to go out. One evening, when he was even later than usual, he found a note in the kitchen, which read, 'Your supper is in the dog.'

What does a footballer do if he splits his sides laughing?
Runs until he gets a stitch.

Two boys were trespassing on the local football pitch when the groundsman came out and bellowed at them, 'Didn't you see that sign?!'
'Yes, but it said "Private" at the top so we didn't like to read any further,' replied the boys.

Final Whistle

'Doctor, doctor, I feel like a referee.'
'Don't be silly, you must have some friends.'

If you have a referee in
football and an umpire
in cricket, what do you
have in bowls?
Goldfish.

What was the film about referees called?
The Umpire Strikes Back.

What happened when the
referee had a brain transplant?
The brain rejected him.

What do you call a referee wearing
five balaclavas on a cold day?
Anything you like, he can't hear you.

Who hangs out the washing on a football pitch?
The linesman.

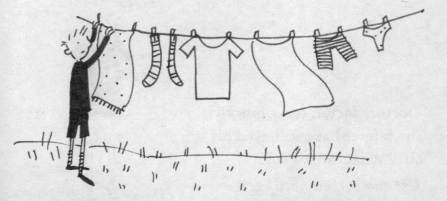

Why did the referee have a sausage stuck behind his ear?
Because he'd eaten his whistle at lunchtime.

A man realized that his new neighbour was a famous football player.
'I've seen you on the TV, on and off,' he said.
'And how do you like me?' asked the player.
'Off,' replied the neighbour.

When is a football coach not a football coach?
When it turns into the ground.

'Doctor, doctor, come quickly! The referee has swallowed his biro! What can we do?'
'Use another one until I get there.'

A football coach-driver went to a garage.
'Can you have a look at my bus? I
think the engine's flooded,' he told the
mechanic.

'Is it on the road outside?' asked the
garage man.

'No, it's at the bottom of the canal,'
replied the coach-driver.

One day when United were playing, the referee
didn't turn up, so the captain asked if there was
anyone among the spectators with refereeing
experience. A man stepped forward.

'Have you refereed before?' asked the captain.

'Certainly,' said the man. 'And if you don't believe
me, ask my three friends here.'

'I'm sorry,' said the captain. 'But I don't think we
can use you.'

'Why not?'

'You can't be a real referee because no real referee
has three friends.'

JOHN: I've driven a football coach for thirty years and never had an accident.

DON: I guess that makes you a wreck-less driver.

Why is a referee like a kettle?

They both whistle when they're hot.

When can a football coach drive on water?

When it goes over a bridge.

CLAUDE: But for Herbert we'd have lost the match today.

MAUD: Is he the striker or the goalie?

CLAUDE: Neither, he's the ref.

Which footballer keeps the house warm in winter?

Ashley Cole.

REFEREE: Will I be able to see right across the pitch with these new glasses?

OPTICIAN: Yes.

REFEREE: That's wonderful! I never could with the old ones.

RACHEL: Three footballers got caught out in the snow, but only two got their hair wet.

LLOYD: Why?

RACHEL: The other one was bald!

Why is a football crowd learning to sing like a person opening a tin of sardines?

They both have trouble with the key.

Which part of a football coach is the laziest?

The wheels, they're always tyred.

DAD: Shall I put the kettle on?

SON: You could, but I think you look all right in your football kit.

Why didn't the conceited footballer wash very often?

Because when the bathroom mirror got all steamed up he couldn't admire himself!

REFEREE: I didn't come here to be insulted!

DISGRUNTLED FAN: Where do you usually go?

FATHER: You mustn't fight, you must learn to give and take.

DENNIS: I did. I gave Danny a black eye and took his football!

MOTHER TO MUDDY
FOOTBALLING SON: You're
pretty dirty, Bobby.
BOBBY: I'm even prettier clean.

Ned was speaking about the
opposing team's striker.
'He's out of this world!' he said.
Ted grinned wryly. 'Our team often wishes he was.'

BILLY: That new striker is a man
who's going places!
WILLY: And the sooner the better!

BEN: I hear that new player's father is an optician.
LEN: Is that why he keeps making such a spectacle
of himself?